MEMORIES BURNT ON PAPER
BY SHRIYA CHATURVEDI

SHRIYA CHATURVEDI

Worldwide Published by
Pendown Press

PENDOWN PRESS
An ISO 9001 & ISO 14001 Certified Co.,
Regd. Office: 2525/193, 1st Floor, Onkar Nagar-A,
Tri Nagar, Delhi-110035
Ph.: 09350849407, 09312235086
E-mail: info@pendownpress.com
Branch Office: 1A/2A, 20, Hari Sadan, Ansari Road,
Daryaganj, New Delhi-110002
Ph.: 011-45794768
Website: PendownPress.com

First Edition: 2023

ISBN: 978-93-5554-531-2

Layout and Cover Designed by Pendown Graphics Team
Printed and Bound in India by Thomson Press India Ltd.

I dedicate this book to anyone
around the world who has felt alone
in a crowd full of people.

CONTENTS

Hi, i'm Shriya or birdie as my loved ones call me

I am a psychology student in my junior year of high school and an utterly confused teenage girl. I write, I dance, and I like to act. I love fashion and the rain and the moon and animals, but most of all, I love the people I'm surrounded with, but it wasn't always like that. I was bullied badly by my friend group, and it wasn't easy. The one person who got me through it was my boyfriend at the time. Unfortunately, things didn't end well, and I was going through a very hard time, and I have no shame in admitting that it was bad, I got admitted to rehab for self-harm. That's when I started writing. This book is about my fight with myself, the fight that only my mirror knows. It is about more than one kind of love, romantic but platonic, family, self-love and toxic love as well.

I'm still fighting to find myself and heal, so maybe if you're going through something similar, you can find comfort in my writing and I hope you do.

Reach out, it helps.

I want you to know that no matter where you are or who you're with, you're worth fighting for. It may not be someone else fighting for you, but there's always one person, yourself. Your younger self who looks up to you, your body that's fighting to save you, your mind that just needs your support, and your future that you still have to live for. I love you, I may not know you, but I know that once and if I do get to have the pleasure to know you, I will love you. You may have messed up, but hey, so have I, and so has everyone else. So don't be too hard on yourself; you're worth the wait, I promise.

So enjoy my memories burnt on paper, I hope they make you feel something, anything.

-THE BEGINNING-

There once lived a girl called Saige, with straight, brown hair and a childish smile. She loved dancing and dressing up. She would dance in the rain and hug everyone she met because she wished they all felt loved.

She met a boy named Vincent, with hazel eyes and a uniquely deep voice. He seemed like someone who would always do the right thing without thinking twice. There was a wise aura about him despite being ten years old. Years went by, and they remained friends through thick and thin, he was her shoulder to cry on, and she would fight the world for him. He fancied her best friend, Trinity, though and soon, it became young love.

-4 years later-

The friendship of 9 years between the young women, Trinity and Saige, came to a halt due to a heartbreaking night of words that made Saige bleed and Trinity turn away. It was difficult of course, but Saige was excited as it was a special day. It was Vincent's birthday, and they hadn't spoken for 3 months due to the spread of the pandemic. She called him up, hoping to surprise him, and they spoke for hours. As she found out that the young love between the hazel-eyed couple, Trinity and Vincent, had broken apart due to unforeseen circumstances, a small part of her that she had kept hidden for 4 years started to quietly bloom. Saige knew she had to conceal these feelings, but how? Not a clue in the world.

-UNREQUITED LOVE-

"I've stepped back and watched you burn with the fire she puts in your heart, the way you talk of each other is more than a young love, it's two old souls, a twin flame, it's beautiful, but sometimes I wish I were a part of it, next to you, I like to pretend we're together to feel at peace, to feel secure in my own mind."

1

UNSPOKEN THOUGHTS

He's so beautiful, with his calm nature and playful aura. I feel the kindness in his hazel eyes. Oh no….he caught me admiring him.

She's so sweet, with her quirky jokes and relentless charm. I understand why he'd want to hold those soft hands of hers.

Every day I try to listen to him talk because I'm a friend, just a friend…. I'm not a girl to him, just someone he can rely on, but I'm happy for them, believe me, I am. They're my chosen family, and I would pull the trigger on my own head for them.

I watch him, doe-eyed, as he watches her, tenderhearted. It's difficult because everything about us is the same. Her and I think the same, talk the same and act the same, we're best friends, and yet I can't help but compare myself to her beauty, wondering if he'd love me, had I looked a little more like her too?

2

FORBIDDEN ADMIRATION

White as my lies
Sweet as your smiles
I mustn't let myself fall deeper into your hazel eyes
Gray as the clouded sky
One word we'll never say, goodbye
Listening to you talk of her, this is why I must hide

I don't feel jealous, of course, why would anyone think that?
It's just her hair, her skin, her everything that I wish I had
Your kindness is unreal, your smile is the sun
I just hope you love her because I want your happiness if she's the one
Hold her like you mean it, she'll give it right back to you
One day you might even tell your kids you loved her as you grew

Keep her in your hoodies and tell her you love her
As much as I wish you would, don't let things go from "are" to "were"
This hurts to say, but she's wonderful, and so are you
So don't let go, don't regret the relationship you threw
Your aura is orange, a little sweet and a little playful
I'll love you both and be happy, I know I'm able

     Forbidden admiration

3

STARTING FRESH

Hi there, it has been a while, tell me how you've been

I want to act cool, but I've steadied myself a million times for this scene

Why does it still sound so sweet, your voice?

It still makes my heart beat slower, between all the noise

You're thinking of how things used to be, when she was all you'd see

It's all gone now, *now you're tender hearted in front of me*

But make sure that you eat well, I promise this will pass

You and her were so good, but it didn't last

I sincerely do mean it, I'll stand at your door

Stand guard at your heart, you deserve happiness and more

So please just don't say those words, please don't?

Whenever you say it, you hurt me, you don't know

When you say that you love me, no point you see

You don't know what kind of love it has always been for me

-STOLEN GLANCES-

"your beauty, your giggles, we're kids, but we're young enough to enjoy our moments and old enough to love each other with everything we've got, so let's not be scared, let's turn this into something beautiful."

1

SAVED ON MY LAPTOP

My phone gets taken away at 11 pm, but I sneak my laptop to talk to you all night

We text and laugh, and blush, and everything feels just right

Sometimes you tell me things you've never told anyone

And I just want to hug you because you're the one

I hope this becomes what I want it to

Because I don't know what I'd do without you

I miss seeing your smile every day

When I played with your ear till you'd sleep on my shoulder and my feelings would be given away

So you can keep me in your hoodies and tell me what you feel

So that we can break this distance through a screen

I'll let you be my everything for eternity

As long as you promise you feel the same for me

2

MAYBE THIS COULD BE REAL

It's June 20th, and we've been talking for almost a month

Things seem to be going good, and I think I'll tell you once

My head is pounding, and heartbeat is fast, Viviann says I should do it

"Do you want to hang out sometime?" no… "I like you! I admit"?

Ah, forget it. I can't do this I don't want to lose our friendship

I'll just tell you I used to like you 4 years ago.

Maybe that'll open up a conversation for more

Okay, I said it, what happens now

Never mind you just said that's cute, I don't understand how

I really thought this would happen, but maybe I was wrong

Now I'm writing down my feelings in form of song

I crumple pages of my diary and stare at the wall, disappointed

Maybe we're better as friends, maybe that's what your point is.

I'll just go to sleep and think about it tomorrow

~~"goodnight<3"~~ no, that's too much, or maybe I'm just sorrow?

3

WARM WEDNESDAY NIGHT IN JUNE

It's been 4 days since I lost hope, and things haven't been different

The blushing and laughing at 2 am in all innocence

I'm confused this feels like something more, but what if it isn't

What if, even after 4 years I'm still not sufficient?

For you to look at me as something more than a best friend

Enough to give me a part of your heart, enough time to spend

Wait, you just texted me saying the feeling was mutual

You've been typing a long time, more than usual

I can't believe the words I'm reading. I'm so overjoyed

"Saige Celeste, will you be my girlfriend?" my hands are joined

"YES, YES, YES" I can't believe this is finally happening

Is it possible that I'm asleep and all this I'm imagining?

God, I love you so much I'm crying happy tears

Thank you, thank you for destroying all my fears

-ENAMOUR-

"You paint me purple, with love, with trust, with every word you say, this love is our baby, and I wish to raise it with the purple, I live you, I will always live to love you, I live you."

1

YOUNG LOVE

I'm falling in love with you, and you're falling in love with me
One of the best feelings I could ever feel

These lego necklaces help me keep a piece of your heart with me
Accidental but inevitable, you are my destiny

I love the way your voice goes up an octave when you say hi to me
The way I look at you and your heart eyes waiting for me to see

Our conversations where time doesn't matter to me
I'm calm, I'm thinking of the good things I'm where I need to be

Your hands intertwined in mine, and it feels like no time has passed to me
I feel like a weight got lifted off my shoulders. I feel free

Your glistening eyes under the sunlight are so beautiful to me
If I could marry you right now, I'd be down on one knee

It took us 5 years to get here, I'm grateful, I am, trust me
When I hear your voice, all I hear is tranquility

2

DANCING WITH YOUR HAND IN MINE

My hand in yours, my head on your shoulder

Slow dancing with dimmed purple lights and laughing, talking of when we get older

That smile sneaks up on your lips

Then your sunlight meets my moonlight, and you hug me like an eclipse

You teasing me about how I smell like my favorite spicy fries

You being there when I need you to handle all my cries

You're better than anyone I've ever met before

Because you're truly mine as I am truly yours

You're on call with me a little too late at night

I laugh a little too loud, and I'm worried someone will hear me, I don't know who might

So you try and make me laugh louder, and it works

And I get yelled at by dad, you seriously feel like a curse

3

NEVER TRULY GONE

I love your voice, your eyes, your smile, your hands, your soul and everything about you

You love my writing, dance and everything about me too

I make cute wallpapers that you're too scared to use

And then I sneak out of the house, saying I'm meeting my friends to cover up our ruse

We spend an hour like not a minute has passed

And then I tell you everything about my past

You hold me tight and say you'll never let go

And I believe you, but maybe you're lying, and I don't know

Whatever, you love me, and that's not a lie

All that matters rather than lows are the highs

So I hold on a little longer and promise to put you first

And I promise to love you through better and worse

–THE CHAOS IN MIDST
OF THE LAUGHTER–

All was going well in their world, Saige and Trinity had mended fences, and the hazels, as she liked to call Vincent and Trinity, were friends. Saige finally felt like she and Vincent were in a good place, the cherry on top was that the wounds 2021 left on Saige were finally turning into scars until a familiar face came around. Aiden was Saige's first love, as she would call it. As you can probably guess, things didn't end well between Saige and Aiden and the last time they spoke, harsh words were exchanged (to say the least). Aiden wished to apologize and make things right, and Saige, in an attempt to be mature, agreed. But how mature can a 15-year-old girl who gets her feelings jumbled up often really be?

The pair were talking often, and to no one's surprise, Vincent wasn't too happy about this. He was Saige's well-wisher, and naive little Saige probably should've listened to him, but alas, then it wouldn't be quite the story it is now. Nostalgia was in the air, and Saige wasn't quite sure what she felt. This broke Vincent's heart as he had given his all to this relationship for 2 years, which is remarkable for any young love of this generation. Aiden strung Saige along, and she confused her nostalgia for real feelings. I did tell you he was her first love, didn't I?

Within a week, the end of Vincent and Saige's relationship was visible to everyone around, and on a cold Wednesday evening in February, everything took a turn for the worse.

-THE DOWNFALL-

"Fell from cloud 9, you rained down upon the lake with tears, and I drowned in the lake with memories and voices of yesterday."

1

HESITATION

I'm seeing your smile drop as I turn my head away in shame

My sister warned me against this, but I guess my beloved emotion is pain

I tell him, "We didn't talk last night for the first time in the history of our relationship."

I try to act normal as the words he probably never should've said again escape his lips

Then I convince myself that I'll be fine, and with the red flags of our interactions, I paint my lips scarlet red

It dawns upon me that I'm not being true to my emotions, but time can't be turned, nor words unsaid

I know it's painful for you to see me do this, but I wish not to lie to you. I wish to be honest

I still love you with all my heart, and I always will that I can promise

Another chance to someone in the past sounds like a mistake waiting to happen

But I can feel a connection, his words as smooth as satin

I'm conflicted. I do not want to hurt either, I'm not quite sure how to continue

In the Bermuda triangle of my mind, I'm bound to doom no matter what I do

2

HAUNTED

I'm in way too deep, and there's no turning back

Just talking to him makes me think of everything I lack

He's being nice, and it feels like he's changed

But it's the same thing from years ago, just words rearranged

There's nostalgia for sure, but I miss the love that made me feel safe

Safe and sound, but I thought too little or too much

You gave me love letters, but I tore them all up

He's perfect on paper, but his words of pencil can be erased and manipulated

My head is pounding, why are emotions so complicated?

I miss you, I miss you, I miss you, I miss us

But I've hurt you too much to consider this a matter we can discuss

Trust is fragile and easy to break

Once gone, hard to earn back, no matter what are the stakes

I put our love in the spotlight, but now it feels like an interrogation lamp

Lady and the tramp, only lady got way over her head and ended on an endless tramp

3

HEARTSICK

You've been down I don't know how to feel

But something about this nostalgia feels so real

What if I let myself go in the other direction?

What if, after all these years, I fail your expectations?

Things are going south, this isn't what I wanted

I'm starting to fade out of the hellhole I started

Sealed my fate with a forbidden kiss

Snapped into reality, fell into a dark abyss

I realize what just happened there is no going back now

I don't want to lose you, I love you, and I will let you down

I keep hurting you, maybe you're better off without me

Love is blind, and so were we, but the blindfolds off, and you can now see

But I hope someday you see that we're both wounded soldiers shot in our heads

In the battlefield of teenage love, in the silence of our empty minds and beds

-HEARTBREAK-

"Once upon a time, I was the one who stitched up your tapestry, your fragmented vision of yourself, but now that you're gone, I can't bring myself to accept that it's truly over, I tore your tapestry back down, and re broke your heart in a kaleidoscope of pain."

1

HOW IT GOES

It started with glowing hearts and muffled laughs a little too late at night, and it ended with dark thoughts and loud cries a little too early in the morning. I wish I'd known my actions a little better because then I wouldn't have lost you before I found what love really meant. You were there for me in my highs and lows, and now I'd do anything to get rid of this high heart rate and low will to live. Sometimes I forget about you, and everything starts to feel alright, but then it hits me out of the blue, and suddenly my whole world is painted with a dark hue.

You said your heart ached whenever you thought of me, and that made my stomach drop six feet. You were a mystery till you were not, and I was perfect until I was not. It feels almost as if I'm a glass half full, I fill in the rest with my tears, and they start to pour over. We were happy, and we loved each other. Little did I know that the exclamations of love would turn into a million little doubts in your head and a billion question marks in mine, which would then end in a full stop in front of our barely completed story?

2

FATALISTIC REALITY

My tears blurring out, and so are my emotions

Realizing I was the person you once loved holding

Like the moon phases, I had all of you, then little by little, it turned to none

Maybe the cycle will repeat itself ~~because I know you're the one,~~ but I know there's no one.

Had an epiphany a little too late

Wanted to come back, but your love turned to hate

Tugging at my hair, memories burnt in my mind

The train to our future left me behind

I really gotta accept it, but I'd never known

That love would end in being shaken to the bone

Its dark outside, and the summer of love's over

And every time you talk to me, you grow a little bit colder

I'm colder, I'm scared of losing you, I always have been

Nightmares crawling, trees falling, all lights have now dimmed

3

ODE OF THE INEVITABLE

My breath shaky, my heart breaking

I always wonder why we're so ill-fated

June was happiness, December went wrong

Now I pour out my heart to you in form of song

I can make it better, please try to believe me

I urge you, I plead you, not to leave me

Your soft exhale, your heart breaking

All you can think of is how I kept you waiting

January was calm February broke you

Now you've finally ended it in time overdue

You don't trust me you can't believe me

Your head is clouded while I beg you not to leave me

I was in a field of dandelions they all blew away

It was the way you said my name now I fall asleep crying cause we didn't stay

Your laugh, your smile is gone I dug my own grave now, in it, I lay

-REGRET-

"You gave me your all, and I adored it, but I couldn't
give you anything but pain, my eyes are sore with
tears, and my lips are red with regret."

1

FOREVER IN MY STORY

They were as beautiful as the sound of a chuckle after a breakdown
They were as cozy as a cottage in a small little town
They could've had it all, could've been the heads with crowns

They were as serene as the orange sky after rain
Till she broke hearts when she was mad and he couldn't fix things back up again
Tried to stay calm, couldn't let things go to vain

They could've had it all, but she pulled the trigger on his head instead of her own
Crestfallen, she sat with a guilty conscience on her throne
Drowned in her tears as she slowly turned to stone

They could've had it all because they were as beautiful as one could ever be
Giggling while slow dancing, beautiful sounds of glee
 He sits amongst the clouds, mourning her while she drowns in her very own sea

2

TORN HEARTS

Someday I hope we can go back to when this started.

Some days I wish I hadn't taken you for granted.

The feelings were strong, but the trust was *weak.*

Somehow I ruined a love that ran deep in less than a week.

With every single day, the trust only *lessened.*

Finally, it ended with two broken hearts and one common lesson.

I thought my *lie* would save our peace of mind

But now we *lie* awake on cold empty nights.

I think I've figured out how to *let this* go now,

I need to *let you let me* go even though it rips my heart out.

In *sometime,* come back to me when your vision's not distorted

Sometimes, I wish we could go back to before this started

3

CEASEFIRE ON MY MIND

It would've been too perfect had we worked out

Our future on a golden platter, but we broke it all down

I'd like to think the blames not all mine to keep

Just so I could get one night of peaceful sleep

Together for better or worse, but it all got too much

For a while, it was perfect on paper, but we tore it all up

Felt like sketching up a masterpiece, but somethings not quite there yet

Making all these memories only to one day forget

You're about to fall asleep, but that one thought keeps you scared

You say something wishing for a reply that shows a little care

Reading through old texts, breaking like every promise

Thoughts hit, maybe forever for you is not us

It would've been too perfect had we worked out

Just know that I loved you throughout

-UNREQUITED LOVE...
ONCE AGAIN-

"I remember when we went through it all only to come out stronger, I'd hoped this time would be the same, but I guess mistakes lead to consequences, and it's time I accept that but I don't want to, so I'll read through our texts again and hug my pillow pretending it's you just to feel at home in my own body."

1

FIRE AND WATER

Our love was like fire and water, me, who would always burn for you and you, who would always melt at the thought of me

Our love was like fire and water, the little moments like when a smile crept up on my lips while gazing at you, who looked so ethereal while holding our necklace in your artistic hands. The very hands whose fingers always found their way to stroke my cheeks during gentle hugs. Our arguments where I would break down into tears, and your arms, like an *ocean,* always pulled me in and calmly drifted me to the shore.

Our love was like fire and water, maybe in another lifetime, we could cordially exist, maybe we could even fall in love again

But for now, my cheeks will *burn* red whenever I see you, and I'll silently *drown* in your eyes because admiring you from afar is all I can do.

For now, I'll replay the memories in my mind and try to fall asleep, hoping that when I wake up, I'll have traveled back to a time when you hadn't left, leaving me a bag of guilt to keep.

Our love was like fire and water, and in the end, my fire burned both of us with no hesitation.

2

LEGO NECKLACES

I've fallen in love with you, and you've fallen out of love with me. I once smiled at your every text, but now I'm left helpless since your once doe-eyed gaze is suddenly cold and loveless. The matching lego necklace is still around my neck while you've broken yours like our broken promise of forever. It was a dreamy love, dusty diaries, coy smiling. I dream of it now because whenever I see you, the silence between us is louder than any laughs we ever shared. I guess you never know when the other person will hit the brakes because loving has a limit, and you've crossed it. You wish not to see this, you wish not to watch how I've fallen in love with you, and you're out of the woods without me

3

ALL FOR NOTHING

I gave you my word, my soul, my being

I try to talk, but every conversation, you're fleeing

You ripped yourself out of the painting I drew

There's so many things that I wish I could just undo

This hurts me to say, but I'll watch from the side aisle while you're on stage

Romeo and Juliet but

Instead of us, the love died, and my heart's in a cage

Just make sure that you eat well, I hope that this does pass

You and I were beyond beauty, but we didn't last

I really do mean it, I hope you're good

You deserve happiness, and more than I understood

So please don't say the three words, please don't

It hurts you, and it hurts me, we both know

When you say that you love me, what's the use?

You don't know that for me, our love is forever, no matter what we've been through

-SELF-LOATHE-

"I think sometimes I look in the mirror and my body with cuts and bruises, my face with smudged lip stain and tears of mascara feels more beautiful than my smiling self."

1

SONNET OF A LOST SOUL

I know I'm young, but the pain's getting old

I can't do it I can't do this any more

People keep dying people keep leaving

When is it my turn to start breathing?

My mother is trying her best to stay strong I'm sitting here watching her while I do everything wrong

I want to change I promise I do

Slowly I'm turning from *yellow to blue*

My fears are becoming real, and I don't know if I'll survive

I stained my wrists red in an attempt to die

There she goes, she's yelling, she's grabbing my hair and pulling me down

She's scared of losing me, and I'm scared of who I've become now

Written my suicide note, said my goodbyes

All that is withering one day dies

My loved ones deserve better, but I'm incapable of change

Somehow it only gets worse with time and with age

2

LORD SAVE ME

Shaking hands and red eyes

My world full of horror and lies

"One day, everyone dies"

They say thinking they are being wise

A mind that wishes to die

A body that fights to survive

How to convince both to end this life?

Every day I cry silent cries

Hurting my arms or my so-called big thighs

Anxiety is caring too much

But depression cares too little

Subconsciously, my hands always fiddle

Living in hell while people tell me I'm in heaven

Holding out hope, wishing upon 11:11

Sometimes I wonder if I really wish to wake up

Everything I have or had turned on me, like my luck

I think I know now that I'd like to never get up again

Stay under the covers, praying to start again from where it all began

3

AM I A CRIMINAL?

They say time never comes back, but June's here to haunt me again

Those laughs of our past and the memories of my sins

They say the present is a gift, in which case how should I return it?

Because I'd rather not be in debt to the future, which apparently doesn't exist

They say I should reach for the moon to land among the stars

But I reached for the moon of your heart and landed with only scars

In some way or another, these scars form my own constellations

That's a beautiful thought but a bittersweet observation

Because, in the end, this makes me a criminal doesn't it?

My red wrists and blue lips are proof of the crimes I commit

They say the law is blind, but the laws of society lead all eyes to me

My cries for help aren't heard, so it's deaf, not blind, really

We've all wanted to quit it all at some point or the other

So are we really all that different under all the layers and covers

-THE END IS JUST
THE BEGINNING-

Well, if that wasn't a roller coaster of emotions, I'm not sure what would be, but after months of back and forth. Saige was finally hitting the realization that she could not and must not grieve the breakup for much longer. She was still quite weak in front of Vincent, but ever since she cut Aiden off, she felt lighter. She had many to support her. Her family, her best friends (Trinity, Neveah and Viviann), her sisters (Anne. Amelia and Lily) and her pet (Luna) all had her back through this. Now she just had to fight her inner guilt and shame. It was June once again, only this time things weren't nearly as flowers and rainbows as they were 2 years ago, and she had a lot more to work through on her own, but after nights of hoping for impending doom, our sweet shade of green finally found peace, like the meaning of her name. Saige thought her story would start and end with unrequited love, but what she didn't realize is that she lived before him, she lived loving him, and she would very well live without him.

She would still cry sometimes, enough to submerge a whole town with her tears, but eventually, she'd calm down, and everything would go back to being okay. She was growing stronger every day, and trust me when I say no one thought she would live to see that day. Point being it was tough, and when she had to face Vincent every day and smile like nothing had happened, she would go into the bathroom and break down each time, but I think we underestimate our Saige. She could and would be strong in front of all of them one day, and the day she did, our story would end with the happy ending that no fairytale could replicate…

But hey, it's not actually the end is it? Because this is just a section of her story, she'll add a chapter and another chapter because this is just the beginning.

Our story is yet to finish.

-ACCEPTANCE-

"I miss you, but you're not my whole life, you're a
chapter in the story of my soul, you're beautiful, but
the you in my memories doesn't exist anymore, so I'll
keep you in my memories and love me of now."

1

DAWNING

Nights I stayed up crying

Days and days of denying

Cried buckets of tears to put out the fire that burned us both

Reminiscing over what we had, our relationship like an oath

Maybe sometimes distance is exactly what we need

When the tears start to pour over when you're in way too deep

Together for better or worse doesn't make you a saint or a god

One train left, but there's always another to take me to dawn

I still care for you, might shed a tear or two sometimes

Since you saw the good in me through the worst of my crimes

But that love can be cherished in the past while looking to the future

She'll love you for who you are now, just how I loved you for who you were

Nights I will stay up laughing with someone new

Days and days you'll spend happily with her too

2

THE BEAUTY OF DISTANCE

I loved you, and as I promised, I still do

I'm getting stronger, but I fall everytime I see you

It's like a tunnel that I just cannot seem to get through

But I have to learn to un-need to reverse my "yellow to blue"

I see you happy, and though many think I'm bitter, that's not necessarily true

People come and go, we're not all the same as we once knew

You once ripped yourself out of the painting I drew

Somehow behind the paper you ripped was a peaceful view

I wasn't unhappy with you, together we flew

But I think this lesson is the reason I grew

I used to write letters with no address to send them to

But now I just write them to myself, the me that's new

I'm learning to love them, my scars that are temporary tattoos

I think I'd be comfortable enough to love myself without a redo

My tears died out in time overdue

Thought I wouldn't make it, but this June got me over you

The beauty of distance

3

BLACK SWAN

I turned sixteen today, a day I always pictured with you by my side

But I see our pictures from months ago, and I see a ghost in place of you tonight

All these people, all this crowd, it doesn't feel the same, but it feels like home

These people love me and care for me, I'm happily shaken to the bone

We all dressed up in black today, mourning my old, sad self

I'll let go now, I'll accept and move on for me, not anybody else

My once sore and teary eyes and now bright and clear

And it's for the sake of my happiness, for the ones I dear

I didn't think I would reach this point

But standing amongst the cheer, I felt so spoilt

In the best way possible, I was surrounded by yellow auras

For a second, I could go back to before us

For a day, I didn't miss you so bad

Now in a year, I'm not going to remember the bad times we had

Because frankly, I don't need you to live on

All I need is myself in a room full of white sheep, I'm a black swan

-HEALING-

"What if I let everything go, start fresh, paint my own portrait with pain in beauty, make my scars into my own unique tattoos?"

1

MY OWN CONSTELLATIONS

In front of my eyes, there's only the dark. Even my heartbeat is so unknown

Face you once again, fear-stricken glare, sometimes I just want to break the mirror and my clone

Sometimes loving someone else is much easier than it is to love yourself

And the standards that you set for yourself are much higher than for anyone else

That cycle, once you break it, your life, you might save it

Smile at the mirror instead of looking like you hate it

Maybe the reason for my falling was to land amongst the stars

And all those cupid arrows will find me from afar

The me back then, the me right now, the me from this moment on

My hands, my face, my smile, my trace, this path I'm set upon

I have reasons I should like me

But greater are the reasons I should fight me

But maybe if I can fight myself, I can fight anyone else

So put on the damn boxing gloves till everyone can tell

You're not alone you've got yourself

The one person that truly matters because they're with themselves

2

AMARE TE STESSO

Amare te stesso, love yourself

The moment you put your worth into someone else, you've lost yourself

Because they could walk out any moment, and you're all by yourself

You can love someone else, they'll be loving the mask you put on because you're never yourself

Amare te stesso, hold on to the memories

Keep them but remind yourself to burn the ones that burn down your tapestry

None of this would've happened so casually

You've never been alone because you've had yourself rationally

Amare te stesso, learn to let go

Sometimes it's better to let someone go

I used to get upset over my woes

But sometimes, it's better to let your heartbeat slow

So my love, *Amare te stesso,*love yourself

Because your beauty shines through when you're confident in yourself

When you speak in front of a crowd and just show yourself

When you make silly jokes and feel happy about yourself

3

TRIBUTE TO HER

This is a tribute to her, the one who hurts herself when she gets mad

The one who lets herself shut down in the moment completely when she's sad

The one who calls up everyone crying to find a moment of peacefulness

The one that convinces herself to lose every fight because she's "reasonless"

The one who snorts every time she laughs

The one who smiles and for the people, that matter, writes paragraphs

The one who's a little naive

The one who hides her smile under her sleeve

The one who's trying her best to be confident in the clothes she wears

The one who's doing her best to ignore all the stares

The one who tries to cover herself up with makeup

The one who never feels like she's enough

This is a *tribute to me,* the one who didn't think she'd breathe till now

The one I want to look at and bow

The one who handles her anxiety attack and then smiles like it's no big deal

The one who should care a little for herself, care a little for me

-WORLD OF YESTERDAY,
LOVE OF TOMORROW-

"What is love? It doesn't have to be romantic, and forcing romantic love to include all types isn't fair, so let's celebrate the other kinds of love while accepting the world we lived in yesterday."

This chapter is one that is very close to my heart. I wanted to write this chapter to thank all the people and things that helped me through a very difficult time in my life. If I'm the moon, they are the sun for me because I couldn't possibly shine without them. Thank you. I love you with all my heart <3000.

1

THE PRETTY RED LEAF IN AUTUMN

With beautiful hair and rosy lips and cheeks, the way you shine

You can tell what I feel before it's on my mind

Your soft hands, your beauty ethereal

Your words are gold, and your voice is surreal

Oh, my precious Trinity

I love you till infinity

When you laugh with that sneering look on your face

Your one look makes me giggle on my worst days

You teach me to care for my physical and mental form

Your peachy aura and the hugs that are so warm

Oh, my darling Trinity

I love you for infinity

Your silly remarks about the littlest of things

Your gallery full of me, if you're my autumn, then I'm your spring

Our convivial moments since 2011, with every word we shared, I promise we'll always stay the same

Our moments go further than time till the majority of my heart that you've now claimed

Oh, my love, Trinity

I love you beyond infinity

2

INNER CHILD

Oh, mother, sixteen years since you made me
From then till now, each day, you protect me
The me without you wouldn't be me
I love you till Pluto, and the size of Jupiter is your love for me

Oh, mother, how graceful your hair, a rosy shade of red and brown
How heart-melting, the wrinkles around your eyes when you smile or frown
How elegant, the way you speak, as if you're the head of the crown
How you've fought everything with stout and not once let your head down

Oh, mother, your smile reminds me of sunshine
Your aura radiates kindness, never saturnine
Your strength and trust, I'll forever pray to your shrine
Your silvery voice, your words are sublime

Oh, mother, you are warmth personified
With you in my corner, I've stood fortified
Your hearty laugh, in front of all the pain you hide
Your trust in humanity, it gleams of your inner child

3

THE STAR THAT STRUCK MY HEART

My friends like to call me birdie, well this bird found a home in your nest

Though always dressed like a 75-year-old man, your words always impress

Out of every diamond, jewel and gold coin, you're the one I'll pick from a crest

Your intellect and acumen, with little to no effort, you ace every test

Your long satiny hair and all your kind smiles

Your bronzed skin and comely eyes

Your childlike hands and accent prettier than a million pink skies

Your humor, sensible yet witty enough to calm all my cries

It's been a thrilling 7 years since we first met

You've never once left my side, I'm forever to you in debt

When you have me to put all disputes at rest, why must you fret?

You like mathematical equations, and I would rather read history, our chemistry only we get

Sometimes I feel the era you belong in is Shakespearean

Your taste for fine dining and classical music feels convivial

Once I've shut down, only you know how to pull me out of the oblivion

To the person who always understands me, *I found me in you,* Viviann

     The star that struck my heart

4

A BOND I'D KEEP FOR LIFE

Anne, you're so incredibly strong

Whenever I'm away, it's you I long

Together since day 1, for better and for worse

But sometimes we yank each other's hair out, and you feel like a curse

That's what sisters do, isn't it? I'm an only child, but you feel like a real sibling

If you jumped off a cliff, I'd jump right with you, for you I'm willing

Your tiny nose and gorgeous pink lips

Your clear skin and long artistic fingertips

I love you, I don't say it enough

No matter how much I lie and say I'm fine, you always call my bluff

Thank you for being the sister I needed, I'll be there for life

I might break in front of everyone else, but with you, I feel just fine

In the past, we fought like there was no tomorrow

Over chargers, cookies and the gum, which I didn't want to give you, so I swallowed

In the present, we dance together like there's no one but us in the world

I'll dance like this with you forever, I give you my word

In the future, we'll probably fight over something stupid again

But I'll come back home and hug you everyday, past now and then

Oh Anne, I feel jealous of your beauty

Like an adult, you take on every responsibility and duty

Always there to pick up the broken pieces of my fragile glass-like heart

Then you paint them with your laughter, and the pain starts to look like art

I thank you once again for always defending me to everyone that matters

Let's stay forever young like Alice in wonderland and silly little mad hatters

5

A PIECE OF THE MOON
I CALL MY OWN

My bright-eyed moonshine

The day I saw a picture of you, I took it as a sign

If there's anyone I'd call my child

It'd be you because I melt over your smiles

Your humanistic expressions and tiny paws

Your spotted white and tawny fur, no flaws

I'm still breathing, and you are the cause

I'm so much happier around you than what I was

Luna, you carry yourself with the aura of a tigress

And you look so tranquil when you sleep on my chest

Grabbing your treats and toys running to me, I feel so blessed

Seeing you in pain when I leave for even an hour, the feeling I most detest

I love you if that wasn't already clear

Losing you is the thought I most fear

Without words, you're the one I'm closest to, my dear

The sound of your barks is, to me, the sound of cheer

6

DOE-EYED BEAUTY

11 years old, you stand with your hands on your hips
Never listen to anyone but yourself, never any of my tips
But that's what makes you so special
Behind your stone-like demeanor is a girl that's gentle

The way you care for me and cry at the littlest of my pain
I want to wipe the tears off your face and forever keep those stains
Because that's how much I love you, I'm your big sister, always
With your big eyelashes and luscious hair, things will always go your way

But your interior is even more beautiful because of how genuine you are
Out of everyone in this damn galaxy, you're the brightest star
I know we don't always get along, and maybe it's my fault
But for us to be thicker than blood or oil is all I want

I'll always be there to hand your hand and guide you through everything
If you're stuck in the dark, I'll be your firefly, together we'll be dallying
You can hold me when things go bad or when you just want to cry
I'll work to make everything okay, I might not be enough, but together we'll try

7

THE 7 BOYS THAT STOLE MY HEART

I sit alone, staring at a wall

Open up my laptop as the bright light hits my wet eyes

My heart turns from blue to purple because of you all

I need you, and you save me as time flies

Leader, your intellect cannot be reached by anyone around you, your clumsiness is almost an art

The oldest, you are my moon, my sun and all my stars. I love you beyond this planet till a world afar

The grandpa, your calm aura unless you're yelling and showing your gummy smile, you are truly so smart

The sunshine, your passion, you're the reason I dance, you're the heart of this fandom

The pretty boy, you are perfect the way you are, and you don't need validation from anyone but yourself

My winter bear, my love, seeing you low made my heart sink more than you could ever know

The little one, you're good at everything, and you're so alluring, you teach us to love oneself

My boys, you are the most beautiful people I could ever know, you make my heartbeat slow

The way your love flies to my room, and you stay with me till 4 o'clock

Blue & grey turns to purple, and smiles as time turns to dawn

I listen to your music as sleep starts to knock

I joined you in 2017, you've kept me sane, I'm drawn

    The 7 boys that stole my heart

8

MY SECOND HOME

Though three of you aren't with me today, I'm with you everyday

My love for you exceeds all limits and words one can say

No family, no friends could ever care that way

The greatest pain I've been through is when you passed away

Dadi, I love you beyond limits of the world

The lessons you've taught me that I've learned

Your beautiful *bindi,* gorgeous multi-colored suits and necklaces pearled

You call out my name some hundred times a day to check on me you're always concerned

Baba, drink in your hand, pride on your face

Everyone bowed when they saw your powerful gaze

Your soft heart, your *shayari* never failed to amaze

Not a single soul that could take your place

Nani, the love you always put in the cakes you baked

I remember when I'd worry so much I couldn't sleep till late

Maybe, it was a coincidence, maybe it was fate

But I'm proud that I'm the granddaughter of you, the great

Nana, you were the kindest man that ever walked this earth

I hope you live another great life upon your rebirth

You always supported me in every single matter that was worth

I miss you, so will everyone because that respect you've earned

9

MY LITTLE ONE

You are so strong, Lily
I love your blushed cheeks, really
Your soft voice and loving hugs
Your innocence and harmless bluffs

The way you love food
The way you fight to keep the mood
The way you fight your own body every day
The way you manage to love your life every way

I want to learn from you because you are strength personified
You stood there stopping bullets with your hands and just smiled
Your beauty goes deeper than skin and bone
It goes till your mind and soul

Paper hearts with all your aspirations torn up
But at the age 13 you laugh like it's not too much
You'll shine through this just like you always have
My little one, the future ahead of you has a masterpiece of a plan

My little one

10

MY BIG LITTLE SISTER

2011, a long time it's been

A lot of losses but a lot of wins

Your constantly dyed hair, red, blonde, blue, green

Your sarcastic humor, our telepathy like we're twins

Neveah, you've stuck with me since day 1

We'll stick together till forever our story's just begun

I love you for every scolding and fight

In the end, somehow, you're always right

Our time machine game where you always wanted to be the captain

I'd give in because "hey! I'm younger, let me be caption, now action!!"

You're more mature than anyone our age

And I love you for it, when I got yelled at, I saw your rage

Always protected me, I'll protect you too

Never seen you cry, but I know that you do

You're soft-hearted and beautiful in every way

Your stone-cold aura might scare others but never scared me for a day

11

THE BETTER MAN

Putting blankets on me, you stay up all night

Around you, i somehow convince myself i'm alright

At the end of the day, you put me on top despite every little fight

Doesn't matter who leaves my side because at the end of this tunnel you're my light

Despite every little fight, you fight for me, you're the better man

Each day i grow a little wiser but to you, i'm always your little girl

You dove into the ocean, worked days and found me, your shining little pearl

Sometimes i hate my every feature till i see how similar we are, our cozy little world

Our chubby cheeks, our kind eyes and our noses whose tip has that little curl

That ocean you dove into threw sharks at you but you came out the better man

You work hard and smart, at work you're the most viable

Anything i need, i can come to you for because you're reliable

Your sarcastic jokes, your dog voice around luna, your charm is undeniable

My gratitude towards you is not in thousands or millions or billions, it's unquantifiable

Fought everything to get where you are and you've always been on top, that's the better man

In the school of life, you're the first and most honorable teacher

The pacific ocean might be deep but our connection goes deeper

Feet on the ground but head in the clouds we're both dreamers

Every thought of ours connected, our bond grows through distance but never once weaker

You've lifted me from the ground and flown me to cloud 9, i love you....the better man

The better man

www.ingramcontent.com/pod-product-compliance
Lightning Source LLC
LaVergne TN
LVHW021139200726

843510LV00001B/162